Knit Boutique
Children's Clothing, Accessories, and More

Knit Boutique: Children's Clothing, Accessories, and More
© 2013 by Martingale®

Martingale
19021 120th Ave. NE, Ste. 102
Bothell, WA 98011-9511 USA
ShopMartingale.com

No part of this product may be reproduced in any form, unless otherwise stated, in which case reproduction is limited to the use of the purchaser. The written instructions, photographs, designs, projects, and patterns are intended for the personal, noncommercial use of the retail purchaser and are under federal copyright laws; they are not to be reproduced by any electronic, mechanical, or other means, including informational storage or retrieval systems, for commercial use. Permission is granted to photocopy patterns for the personal use of the retail purchaser. Attention teachers: Martingale encourages you to use this book for teaching, subject to the restrictions stated above.

The information in this book is presented in good faith, but no warranty is given nor results guaranteed. Since Martingale has no control over choice of materials or procedures, the company assumes no responsibility for the use of this information.

Printed in China

18 17 16 15 14 13   8 7 6 5 4 3 2 1

Library of Congress Cataloging-in-Publication Data is available upon request.

ISBN: 978-1-60468-309-7

Mission Statement

Dedicated to providing quality products and service to inspire creativity.

Contents

It's a Baby! Jeans and T-Shirt   5

Scalloped-Edge Jumper   9

Three Hats for Baby   11

Comfy Cozy Cardigan   15

Party-Time Jumper   19

Rock-a-Bye Baby Blanket   21

Hush Little Baby Blanket   23

Baby Talk Pillows   25

Baby Bunny Cuddle Toy   27

Knitting Abbreviations   31

Helpful Information   32

It's a Baby! Jeans and T-Shirt

Inspired by Mr. Green Jeans on the "Captain Kangaroo" show, the green jeans with matching T-shirt will be everyone's favorite outfit when your baby sports this cute combo.

Skill Level
■■□□ Easy

Sizes
To fit: 3 (6, 9, 12, 18) months
Finished chest measurement: 18½ (20, 22, 23, 24½)"
T-shirt length: 11 (11¾, 12½, 13¼, 14)"
Pants length: 14½ (16¼, 17¾, 19½, 21)"

Materials
Yarn: 80% pima cotton, 20% wool worsted-weight yarn (4)
  For T-shirt: Approx 380 yds (all sizes), green solid
  For jeans: Approx 380 (380, 570, 570) yds, variegated green
Needles: Sizes 6 and 7 needles, or size required to obtain gauge
Notions: ½"-wide elastic (enough to go around waist plus 2"), snap tape (optional), 1 button (¾" diameter) for shirt

Gauge
20 sts and 26 rows = 4" in St st on larger needles

Jeans
Jeans are made in two pieces and joined.

One Half (Make 2.)
With smaller needles, CO 53 (53, 59, 59, 59) sts. Work in St st for 5 rows. Knit 1 row on WS to create fold line for hem. Switch to larger needles.
Work 2 rows in St st.
Inc rows: (K1f&b, knit to last 2 sts, K1f&b, K1) every 6 rows 9 (10, 11, 12, 13) times—71 (73, 81, 83, 85) sts.
Work even until piece meas 8 (9½, 11, 12½, 14)" from beg, ending with WS row.
Dec rows: BO 3 sts at beg of next 2 rows. BO 2 sts at beg of next 2 rows. Dec 1 st at each side on next 4 RS rows—53 (55, 63, 65, 67) sts.
Cont in St st until piece meas 15½ (17¼, 18¾, 20½, 22)" from beg, ending with RS row.
Knit 1 row on WS to create fold line for casing.
Work 6 rows in St st. BO all sts.

Finishing
Sew front and back seams.
Sew inseams. (Optional: use snap tape on inseam.)
Fold bottom hem at fold line and sew in place.
Fold top casing at fold line and sew, leaving opening to insert elastic. Insert elastic, overlap ends, and sew tog. Sew opening closed.

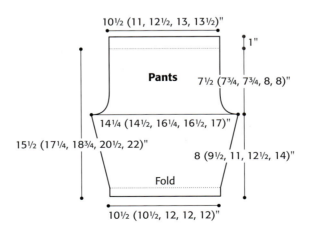

T-shirt

Back
With smaller needles, CO 46 (50, 54, 58, 62) sts. Work in St st for 5 rows. Knit 1 row on WS to create fold line for hem. Switch to larger needles and cont in St st until back meas 6¾ (7½, 8¼, 9, 9¾)" from beg, ending with WS row.

Armholes: BO 2 (2, 2, 3, 3) sts at beg of next 2 rows. Dec 1 st at each side of next 4 (4, 5, 5, 6) RS rows as follows: K1, K2tog to last 3 sts, ssk, K1—34 (38, 40, 42, 44) sts. Cont in St st until back meas 10 (10¾, 11½, 12¼, 13)" from beg, ending with WS row.

Beg neck shaping: K13 (14, 15, 15, 16), BO 8 (10, 10, 12, 12) sts, finish row.

Left neck: Purl 1 row. BO 3 sts at neck, knit to end. Purl 1 row. BO 1 st at neck on EOR 2 times—8 (9, 10, 10, 11) sts. BO all sts.

Right neck: With WS facing you, attach yarn at neck edge, BO 3 sts at neck, purl to end. Knit 1 row. BO 1 st at neck on EOR 2 times—8 (9, 10, 10, 11) sts. Work until back meas 11¾ (12½, 13¼, 14, 14¾)" from beg to top of shoulder. BO all sts.

Front
Work as for back, including armhole shaping. Cont in St st until front meas 8¾ (9½, 10¼, 11, 11¾)" from beg, ending with WS row.

Beg neck shaping: K14 (16, 17, 17, 18), BO 6 (6, 6, 8, 6) sts, finish row.

Right neck: Purl 1 row. BO 2 (3, 3, 3, 3) sts at neck, knit to end. Purl 1 row. *BO 1 st at neck, knit to end. Purl 1 row. Rep from * 4 times—8 (9, 10, 10, 11) sts.
Next RS row (buttonhole row): K2 (2, 3, 3, 3), make 4-st buttonhole, finish row. Purl 1 row. Work 2 rows in St st. BO all sts.

Left neck: With WS facing you, attach yarn at neck edge, BO 2 (3, 3, 3, 3) sts, purl to end. Knit 1 row. *BO 1 st at neck, purl to end. Knit 1 row. Rep from * 4 times—8 (9, 10, 10, 11) sts. Purl 1 row. Omit buttonhole row and work 4 rows in St st. BO all sts.

Sleeves (Make 2.)

With smaller needles, CO 22 (24, 26, 28, 30) sts. Work in St st for 5 rows. Knit 1 row on WS to create fold line for hem. Knit 1 row and inc 1 st at each side—24 (26, 28, 30, 32) sts. Switch to larger needles; working in St st, inc 1 st at each side every 6 rows 6 (7, 8, 9, 10) times—36 (38, 44, 48, 52) sts. Sleeve should meas approx 7¾ (8½, 9¼, 10, 10¾)". If not, work even until it does.

Cap shaping: BO 3 (3, 4, 4, 4) sts at beg of next 2 rows. BO 2 sts at beg of next 8 rows. BO 3 sts at beg of next 2 rows. BO rem sts.

Finishing

Sew short back strap to front strap buttonhole, starting at outside.

Neckband: With RS facing you and starting at left shoulder seam, PU 12 (13, 13, 14, 14) sts across back neck and 20 (20, 20, 22, 22) sts across front—32 (33, 33, 36, 36) sts. Purl 1 row. BO all sts.

Sew on button; baste front to back at shoulder on button side so you can insert sleeve.

Sew sleeves. Sew side seams.

Turn up bottom hem at fold line and sew in place.

Four-Stitch Buttonhole

Work to buttonhole placement, slip stitch purlwise with yarn in front, *slip next stitch with yarn in back from left needle, pass slipped stitch over, and repeat from * three more times. Slip last bound-off stitch to left needle and turn work.

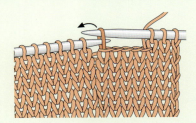

Using cable cast-on method, cast on five stitches.

Slip first stitch with yarn in back from left needle and pass extra cast-on stitch over it to close the buttonhole. Work to end of row.

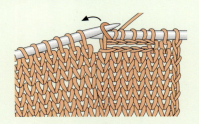

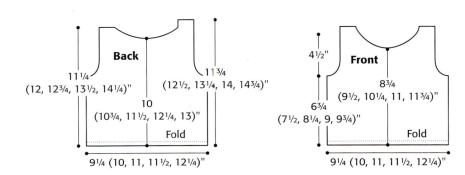

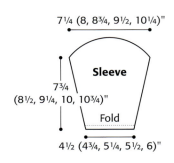

It's a Baby! Jeans and T-Shirt

Scalloped-Edge Jumper

Whatever the occasion, make it even more special for the small fry in your life with this adorable jumper. It's knit in one piece from the bottom up with what's traditionally considered sock yarn.

Skill Level
■■■□ Intermediate

Sizes
To fit: Up to 6 (12, 18, 24) months
Finished chest measurement: 17 (19, 21, 23)"
Length from underarm: 12 (13, 14, 15)"

Materials
Yarn: Approx 330 (375, 435, 500) yds of 75% wool/25% nylon fingering-weight yarn ①
Needles: Size 2 (2.75 mm) circular needles (16" and 24" long), or size to attain gauge
Notions: 1 stitch marker

Gauge
7½ sts and 10 rows = 1" in St st

Skirt
Using 24"-long circular needle, CO 152 (168, 184, 200) sts. Join, being careful not to twist sts, pm to denote beg of rnd.
Rnds 1, 3, and 5: Purl.
Rnds 2, 4, and 6: *K5 (6, 7, 8), ssk, K2tog, K5 (6, 7, 8), YO, K5, YO; rep from * around.
Beg body of skirt:
Rnd 1: *K14 (16, 18, 20), P5, rep from * around.
Rnd 2: *K5 (6, 7, 8), ssk, K2tog, K5 (6, 7, 8), YO, K5, YO; rep from * around.
Rep last 2 rnds until piece meas 4" from beg, ending with rnd 2. For consistent and accurate measuring, measure in garter-stitch sections between scallops.

First dec rnd: *K14 (16, 18, 20), P1, P2tog, P2; rep from * around—144 (160, 176, 192) sts.
Cont as follows:
Rnd 1: *K5 (6, 7, 8), ssk, K2tog, K5 (6, 7, 8), YO, K4, YO; rep from * around.
Rnd 2: *K14 (16, 18, 20), P4; rep from * around.
Rep last 2 rnds until piece meas 7" from beg, ending with rnd 1.
Second dec rnd: *K14 (16, 18, 20), P1, P2tog, P1; rep from * around—136 (152, 168, 184) sts.
Cont as follows:
Rnd 1: *K5 (6, 7, 8), ssk, K2tog, K5 (6, 7, 8), YO, K3, YO; rep from * around.
Rnd 2: *K14 (16, 18, 20), P3; rep from * around.
Rep last 2 rnds until piece meas 10" from beg, ending with rnd 1.
Third dec rnd: *K14 (16, 18, 20), P1, P2tog; rep from * around—128 (144, 160, 176) sts.
Cont as follows:
Rnd 1: *K5 (6, 7, 8), ssk, K2tog, K5 (6, 7, 8), YO, K2, YO; rep from * around.
Rnd 2: *K14 (16, 18, 20), P2; rep from * around.
Rep last 2 rnds until piece meas 12 (13, 14, 15)" from beg, ending with rnd 1.
Fourth dec rnd: *K14 (16, 18, 20), P2tog; rep from * around—120 (136, 152, 168) sts.
Cut yarn. This completes body of jumper. Do not BO; leave sts on needle. Bodice is knitted onto body.

Bodice Border
Using knitted CO, CO 5 sts to left-hand needle. Work applied I-cord as follows: K4, ssk (using 1 st that you just CO and 1 st from sts at top of jumper), sl 5 sts just worked from right needle back to left needle. Rep this process until all sts from skirt top have been worked into border. BO 5 sts.
Sew BO and CO edges tog.

Bodice
With RS facing you and I-cord at top, tip the I-cord slightly downward so you're looking at back of I-cord and WS of bodice. PU 120 (136, 152, 168) sts around back inside edge of I-cord border by picking up the bar before the first stitch of I-cord on the row.

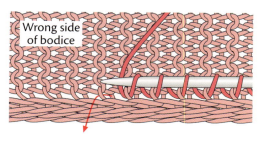

Work bodice as follows:
Rnds 1, 3, 5, 7, and 9: Purl.
Rnds 2, 4, 6, and 8: Knit.
BO sts using same method as for bodice border to make attached I-cord.

Straps (Make 2.)
CO 12 sts.
All rows: K9, sl 3 wyif.
Work in est patt until strap meas 10 (11, 12, 13)" from beg.
BO all sts.

Finishing
Sew straps to inside of front and back bodice along bottom of I-cord. Weave in all ends. Block if desired.

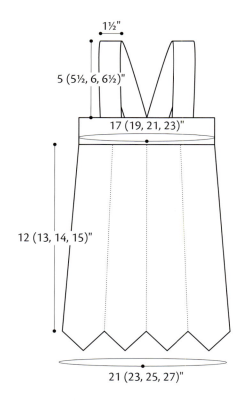

10 Scalloped-Edge Jumper

Three Hats for Baby

As every mother knows, a baby's head gets cold. Slip one of these cozy caps into your diaper bag and you'll have it handy when your little angel needs a hat.

Skill Level
■■□□ Easy

Sizes
Hat A: 13½ (15¾, 18)" circumference
Hat B: 13¾ (15½, 17)" circumference
Hat C: 13½ (15, 16½)" circumference

Materials
All hats call for both a circular needle and double-pointed needles. If you prefer to work hats with double-pointed needles, you will not need a circular needle.

Hat A
Yarn: Approx 123 yards of 100% merino DK-weight yarn 3
Needles: Size 5 circular needle (16") and double-pointed needles or size required to obtain gauge. (If you are making the smallest size, you will need only double-pointed needles.)
Notions: Stitch marker

Hat B
Yarn: Approx 220 yards of 100% merino fingering-weight yarn 1
Needles: Size 3 circular needle (16") and double-pointed needles or size required to obtain gauge
Notions: Stitch marker

Hat C
Yarn: Approx 67 yards of alpaca/wool blend chunky-weight yarn 5
Needles: Size 9 circular needle (16") and double-pointed needles or size required to obtain gauge
Notions: Stitch marker

Gauge
Hat A: 18 sts and 32 rows = 4"
Hat B: 28 sts and 36 rows = 4"
Hat C: 16 sts and 18 rows = 4"

Hat A
Switch to dpns when necessary.
Using circular needle, CO 60 (70, 80) sts. Join into rnd, pm, and work seed-st patt as follows:
Rnd 1: *K1, P1; rep from * around.
Rnd 2: *P1, K1; rep from * around.
Rep rnds 1 and 2 for total of 16 rnds.
Knit 8 rnds.
Work seed-st patt for 8 rnds.
Knit 4 rnds.
Work seed-st patt for 4 rnds.
Knit 1 rnd.
Work dec rnds as follows:
*K8, K2tog; rep from * around—54 (63, 72) sts.
Knit 1 rnd.
*K7, K2tog; rep from * around—48 (56, 64) sts.
Knit 1 rnd.
*K6, K2tog; rep from * around—42 (49, 56) sts.
Knit 1 rnd.
*K5, K2tog; rep from * around—36 (42, 48) sts.
Knit 1 rnd.
*K4, K2tog; rep from * around—30 (35, 40) sts.
Knit 1 rnd.
*K3, K2tog; rep from * around—24 (28, 32) sts.
Knit 1 rnd.
*K2, K2tog; rep from * around—18 (21, 24) sts.
Knit 1 rnd.
*K1, K2tog; rep from * around—12 (14, 16) sts.
Knit 1 rnd.
K2tog until 3 sts rem. Work I-cord on 3 rem sts as follows: *Without turning needle, slide sts to other end of needle, pull yarn tightly around the back, and knit sts as usual. Rep from * for 2". K3tog, pull yarn through last loop, and sew loop to top of hat. Weave in ends.

4½" Hat A
13½ (15¾, 18)"

12　Three Hats for Baby

Hat B

Switch to dpns when necessary.
Using circular needle, CO 96 (108, 120) sts. Join into rnd, pm, and work ribbing as follows:
All rnds: *K1, P1; rep from * to end until hat meas 1½".
Switch to St st (knit all rnds) and work until hat meas 3¼ (3½, 3¾)".
Work dec as follows:
*K10, K2tog; rep from * around—88 (99, 110) sts.
Knit 3 rnds.
*K9, K2tog; rep from * around—80 (90, 100) sts.
Knit 3 rnds.
*K8, K2tog; rep from * around—72 (81, 90) sts.
Knit 2 rnds.
*K7, K2tog; rep from * around—64 (72, 80) sts.
Knit 2 rnds.
*K6, K2tog; rep from * around—56 (63, 70) sts.
Knit 1 rnd.
*K5, K2tog; rep from * around—48 (54, 60) sts.
Knit 1 rnd.
*K4, K2tog; rep from * around—40 (45, 50) sts.
Knit 1 rnd.
*K3, K2tog; rep from * around—32 (36, 40) sts.
Knit 2 rnds.
*K2, K2tog; rep from * around—24 (27, 30) sts.
Knit 2 rnds.
*K1, K2tog; rep from * around—16 (18, 20) sts.
Knit 3 rnds.
K2tog until 3 sts rem. K3tog, pull yarn through last loop, and fasten off.
Weave in ends.

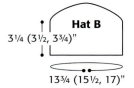

Hat C

Switch to dpns when necessary.
Using circular needle, CO 60 (66, 72) sts. Join into rnd, pm, and work dec as follows:
*K8 (9, 10), K2tog; rep from * around—54 (60, 66) sts.
Knit 1 rnd.
*K7 (8, 9), K2tog; rep from * around—48 (54, 60) sts.
Knit 2 rnds.
*K6 (7, 8), K2tog; rep from * around—42 (48, 54) sts.
Knit even until hat meas 4" from last dec row.
Work dec as follows:
*K5 (6, 7), K2tog; rep from * around—36 (42, 48) sts.
Knit 1 rnd.
*K4 (5, 6), K2tog; rep from * around—30 (36, 42) sts.
Knit 1 rnd.
*K3 (4, 5), K2tog; rep from * around—24 (30, 36) sts.
Knit 1 rnd.
*K2 (3, 4), K2tog; rep from * around—18 (24, 30) sts.
Knit 1 rnd.
*K1 (2, 3), K2tog; rep from * around—12 (18, 24) sts.
Knit 1 rnd.
*K0 (1, 2), K2tog; rep from * around—6 (12, 18) sts.
Knit 1 rnd.
K2tog around until 2 (3, 3) sts rem. K2 (3, 3) tog, pull yarn through last loop, and fasten off.
Weave in ends.

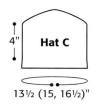

Three Hats for Baby

Comfy Cozy Cardigan

Need a baby gift in a hurry? By making buttonholes on both bands as you go, you could have several of these sweaters made up ahead of time; simply attach buttons to the correct side later.

Skill Level
◼◼☐▷ Easy

Sizes
To fit: Up to 6 (12, 18, 24) months
Finished chest measurement: 18 (20, 22, 24)" when buttoned
Back length: 9½ (10½, 11½, 12½)"
Sleeve length: 6 (6½, 7½, 8½)"

Materials
Yarn: Approx 260 (295, 335, 380) yds of 65% nylon, 35% superwash wool DK-weight yarn **(3)**
Needles: Size 5 (3.75 mm) needles, or size to attain gauge
Notions: 6 stitch markers, 5 stitch holders, 5 buttons (½" diameter)

Gauge
5½ sts and 8 rows = 1" in St st

Cardigans: For a Boy or a Girl?
Since this sweater is knit in one piece with the buttonhole and button bands knit right on, it's important to remember to work buttonhole rows at appropriate measurements. Buttonhole rows have been written with buttonholes worked on both bands. That way you can make this sweater without knowing the sex of the baby and apply the buttons after he or she is born! If you know the sex, simply work buttonholes on one side only—right for girls, left for boys.

Border
Beg at lower edge, CO 106 (117, 128, 139) sts.
Rows 1–4: Knit, marking first row as RS.
Row 5 (buttonhole row): K3, YO, K2tog, knit to last 4 sts, YO, K2tog, K2.
Rows 6–9: Knit.
Row 10 (WS): K6, pm, P16 (19, 22, 25), pm, K12, pm, P38 (43, 48, 53), pm, K12, pm, P16 (19, 22, 25), pm, K6.

Body
Row 1 (RS): Knit.
Row 2: K6, P16 (19, 22, 25), K12, P38 (43, 48, 53), K12, P16 (19, 22, 25), K6.
Rep last 2 rows until piece meas 5½ (6, 6½, 7)" from beg, ending with WS row, and AT SAME TIME work buttonhole row every 16 (18, 20, 22) rows. There will be 8 (9, 10, 11) ridges between buttonholes. (**Note:** When counting rows/ridges between buttonholes, do not count 2 rows/1 ridge where buttonhole was worked.)

Divide for Front and Back
On next row, K28 (31, 34, 37) and place sts on holder to be used later for right front, K50 (55, 60, 65) sts for back, place rem 28 (31, 34, 37) sts on second holder to be used later for left front.

Back
Beg with WS row, cont working in St st while keeping first and last 6 sts in garter st until back meas 9½ (10½, 11½, 12½)" from beg, ending with WS row. Divide sts onto 3 holders:
Holders 1 and 3: 15 (17, 19, 21) sts
Holder 2: 20 (21, 22, 23) sts

Right Front
With WS facing you, return 28 (31, 34, 37) sts from st holder to working needle. Keeping first and last 6 sts in garter st, work in St st until front meas 8 (9, 9¾, 10½)" from beg, ending with WS row and remembering to work buttonholes as required at appropriate intervals.
Neck shaping: K8 (8, 9, 9) sts and place on holder to be used later for neck band. Work across rem sts. Cont in est patt and AT SAME TIME work ssk at neck edge every RS row until 15 (17, 19, 21) sts rem. Work even until front meas same as back, ending with WS row. Join to right-back shoulder using 3-needle BO. (Hold front and back shoulder RS tog, with both needles in LH and pointing toward right. Using third needle, BO 1 st from each needle at same time.)

Left Front
With RS facing you, return 28 (31, 34, 37) sts from st holder to working needle. Keeping first and last 6 sts in garter st, work in St st until front meas 8 (9, 9¾, 10½)" from beg, ending with WS row and remembering to work buttonholes as required at appropriate intervals.

Neck shaping: Work in patt to last 8 (8, 9, 9) sts and place these sts on st holder to be used later for neck band. Cont in est patt and AT SAME TIME work K2tog at neck edge every RS row until 15 (17, 19, 21) sts rem. Work even until front meas same as back, ending with WS row. Join to left-back shoulder using 3-needle BO.

Sleeves

CO 28 (30, 32, 34) sts.

Rows 1–8: Knit, marking first row as RS.

Beg working in St st and AT SAME TIME work incs at each end on fifth row and every fourth row thereafter as follows: K1, M1, knit to last st, M1, K1. Work incs until you have 44 (50, 56, 60) sts.

Work even until sleeve meas 6 (6½, 7½, 8½)", ending with WS row. BO all sts. Work second sleeve in same manner.

Neck Band

Row 1: With RS facing you, sl 8 (8, 9, 9) sts from right-front st holder to needle, attach yarn and PU 14 (15, 15, 16) sts along right neck edge, K20 (21, 22, 23) from back st holder, PU 14 (15, 15, 16) sts along left neck edge, K8 (8, 9, 9) sts from left-front st holder—64 (67, 70, 73) sts.

Rows 2–4: Knit.

Row 5 (buttonhole row): K3, YO, K2tog, knit to last 4 sts, YO, K2tog, K2.

Rows 6 and 7: Knit.

BO all sts on WS.

Finishing

Sew buttons on appropriate side over buttonholes that won't be needed, closing up buttonholes as you do so. Sew in sleeves. Weave in all ends. Block if desired.

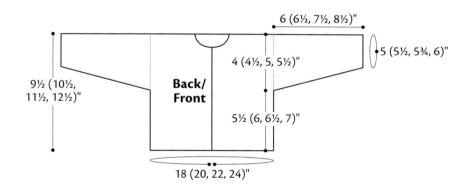

Party-Time Jumper

What little girl wouldn't feel like a princess in this adorable party jumper? It makes special occasions even more special. The I-cord trim adds extra interest to both the yoke and the straps.

Skill Level
■■■□ Intermediate

Sizes
To fit: Up to 3 (6, 12, 18) months
Finished chest measurement: 18 (19, 20, 21)"
Length from underarm: 11 (12, 13, 14)"

Materials
Yarn: Approx 350 (420, 500, 580) yds of 100% merino fingering-weight yarn (1)
Needles: Size 2 (2.75 mm) straight and 24"-long circular needles, or size to attain gauge
Notions: 1 stitch marker, 3 decorative buttons (approx 1" diameter)

Gauge
7½ sts and 10 rows = 1" in St st

Bodice
Using straight needles, CO 17 (20, 23, 26) sts.
All rows: Knit to last 3 sts, sl 3 wyif. Mark first row as RS row.
Work in est patt until piece meas 18 (19, 20, 21)", ending with WS row.
BO all sts. Sew CO edge to BO edge.

Skirt
With WS of work facing you and with circular needle, PU 124 (132, 140, 148) sts under first row of purl loops just above one of the I-cord borders.
Turn work so RS is facing you. Pm to denote beg of rnd. Attach yarn and work skirt section as follows:
Next rnd: *K1, K1f&b in next st; rep from * around—186 (198, 210, 222) sts.
Work in St st (knit every rnd) until piece meas 10½ (11½, 12½, 13½)" from top band or ½" less than desired finished length.

Bottom Border
Rnds 1 and 3: Purl.
Rnds 2 and 4: Knit.
BO all sts purlwise.

Pick-Up Hint
Because I-cord is a horizontal tube, when you pick up stitches along the edge, you're actually picking up the "bar" before the first stitch of I-cord on the row. Hold the bodice with the right side facing you and I-cord at the top. Slightly tip the I-cord down so you're looking at the back of the I-cord and the wrong side of the bodice. Picking up in this manner makes the I-cord pop out more.

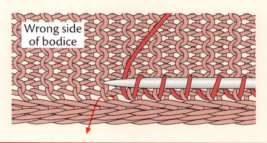

Straps (Make 2.)
Using straight needles, CO 12 (15, 15, 18) sts.
All rows: Knit to last 3 sts, wyif sl 3.
Work in est patt until strap meas 7 (8, 9, 10)".
BO all sts.

Finishing
Sew straps to inside of front and back bodice along bottom of I-cord. Weave in all ends. Block if desired.

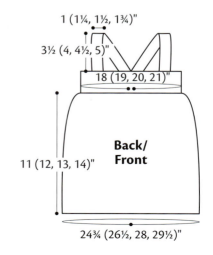

Rock-a-Bye Baby Blanket

Knit in blue or pink (or any color you desire), this soft and snuggly blanket is perfect for those times when a light blanket is just what Baby ordered.

Skill Level
 Easy

Sizes
30" x 30" (30" x 38")

Materials
Yarn: 440 yards *each* of worsted-weight superwash wool yarn in two contrasting colors
Needles: Size 8 circular needle (24") or size required to obtain gauge

Gauge
18 sts and 24 rows = 4"

Blanket
Reversible knitting creates a design that's the same on both sides. To begin, CO using dark yarn; then slide sts to other end of circular needle. Join light yarn and beg reversible patt with row 1. *Do not* cut yarns at ends of rows, but loosely carry them up the side. Don't pull the yarns too tightly or the edge of the blanket will pull in.

With dark yarn, CO 127 (161) sts. Slide sts to other end of circular needle. Join light yarn and beg reversible patt:

Row 1: With light yarn, K1, *P1, K1; rep from *. Turn.
Row 2: With light yarn, P1, *K1, P1; rep from *. Slide.
Rows 3 and 4: With dark yarn, rep rows 1 and 2.
Rep rows 1–4 until blanket is desired length.
Weave in ends.
Block blanket.

Hush Little Baby Blanket

This is a great take-along project that's completely reversible. It's made with superwash wool yarn, which is perfect for Baby—lightweight, warm, comfortable, and extremely washable.

Skill Level
■□□□ Beginner

Size
36" x 36"

Materials
Yarn: Worsted-weight superwash wool yarn (4) in following amounts:
- MC: 660 yards
- CC1: 220 yards
- CC2: 660 yards

Needles: Size 8 needles or size required to obtain gauge

Gauge
18 sts and 24 rows = 4" in garter st

Triangles (Make 4.)
Leave long yarn tails for sewing triangles together. With MC, CO 162 sts and knit 2 rows. Then work as follows:

Row 1: K1, ssk, knit to last 3 sts, K2tog, K1.
Row 2: Knit.

Rep rows 1 and 2 for total of 42 rows or 21 ridges. (2 rows of garter st = 1 ridge.)
Change to CC1 and work rows 1 and 2 for 18 rows or 9 ridges.
Change to CC2 and work rows 1 and 2 until 4 sts rem. On next RS row, ssk, K2tog. Knit 1 row and BO all sts.

Finishing
Start at MC edge and refer to diagram below. Using long tails of yarn to match each section of color, sew pieces 1 and 2 tog; then sew pieces 3 and 4 tog. Sew 2 halves tog to make square. See box below for seaming garter-st edges.

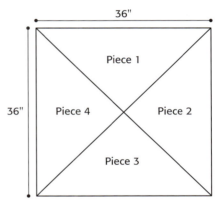

Seaming Garter-Stitch Edges
Look at the garter-stitch edge and you'll see a little knot at the edge of every row. You'll be working into the strand of this knot that wraps around the edge. With a yarn needle and yarn, and working back and forth between the pieces, insert the needle under the strand on one side, and then under the strand on the other side. Draw the yarn through loosely, stitch by stitch; then tighten it up after you've worked four or five stitches.

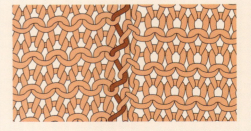

Baby Talk Pillows

It's nice to have something to rest your arm on for support when holding a baby. These pillows squish to a small size and will travel anywhere you go.

Skill Level
■■□□ Easy

Sizes
Pillow A: approx 11" x 13"
Pillow B: approx 12" x 14"
Pillow C: approx 11½" x 13"

Materials
Yarn: For *each* pillow: 220 yds of worsted-weight superwash wool yarn (4)
Needles: Size 8 needles or size required to obtain gauge
Notions: Batting or pillow form* for stuffing

*Purchase pillow form after pillow is complete to ensure good fit.

Gauge
18 sts and 24 rows = 4"

Pillow A

Herringbone Pattern
Multiple of 10 sts
Row 1 (RS): *K9, P1; rep from *.
Row 2: *P1, K1, P8; rep from *.
Row 3: *K7, P1, K1, P1; rep from *.
Row 4: *(P1, K1) 4 times, P2; rep from *.
Row 5: *K3, (P1, K1) 3 times, P1; rep from *.
Row 6: *(P1, K1) 3 times, P3, K1; rep from *.
Row 7: *K1, P1, K3, (P1, K1) twice, P1; rep from *.
Row 8: *(P1, K1) twice, P3, K1, P1, K1; rep from *.
Row 9: *(K1, P1) twice, K3, P1, K1, P1; rep from *.
Row 10: *(P1, K1) twice, P6; rep from *.
Row 11: *K7, P1, K2; rep from *.
Row 12: *P3, K1, P6; rep from *.
Rep rows 1–12 for patt.

Pillow
Front: CO 60 sts. Work herringbone patt 6 times (total 72 rows). BO all sts. If you like, pm every 10 sts to keep track of each patt rep.
Back: CO 60 sts and work in St st until back meas same as front.

Finishing
Place WS of both pieces tog. PU 60 sts at top through both pieces. Work in seed st as follows:
Row 1: *K1, P1; rep from * to end.
Row 2: * P1, K1; rep from * to end.
BO all sts. Rep for opposite (bottom) edge. Weave in ends. Sew rem sides with a backstitch, leaving about 3" opening if stuffing pillow or 8" opening if using pillow form. Fold batting to size of pillow and insert into pillow, or insert pillow form. Sew opening closed.

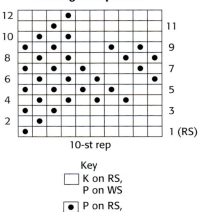

25

Pillow B

Square Pattern

Multiple of 10 + 3 sts
Row 1 (RS): *P1, K1, rep from * to last 3 sts, P1, K1, P1.
Row 2: P1, K1, P1, *K1, P1; rep from * to end.
Row 3: *P1, K1, P1, K7, rep from * to last 3 sts, P1, K1, P1.
Row 4: P1, K1, P1, *P8, K1, P1; rep from * to end.
Rows 5–10: Work rows 3 and 4 another 3 times.
Rep rows 1–10 for patt.

Pillow

Front and back (make 2): CO 63 sts and work patt 8 times; then work rows 1 and 2 one more time (total 82 rows). BO all sts.

Finishing

Place WS of both pieces tog and sew all around with a backstitch, leaving about 3" opening if stuffing pillow or 8" opening if using pillow form. Fold batting to size of pillow and insert into pillow, or insert pillow form. Sew opening closed.

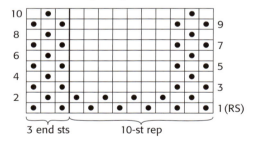

Pillow C

Diamond Pattern

Multiple of 10 + 9 sts
Row 1 (RS): K4, *P1, K9, rep from * to last 5 sts, P1, K4.
Row 2: P3, K1, P1, *K1, P7, K1, P1, rep from * to last 4 sts, K1, P3.
Row 3: K2, P1, K1, *P1, K1, P1, K5, P1, K1, rep from * to last 5 sts, P1, K1, P1, K2.
Row 4: (P1, K1) twice, P1, *K1, P1, K1, P3, (K1, P1) twice, rep from * to last 4 sts, (K1, P1) twice.
Row 5: (P1, K1) twice, *(P1, K1) 5 times, rep from * to last 5 sts, (P1, K1) twice, P1.
Row 6: Rep row 4.
Row 7: Rep row 3.
Row 8: Rep row 2.
Row 9: Rep row 1.
Row 10: Purl.
Rep rows 1–10 for patt.

Pillow

Front and back (make 2): CO 69 sts and work patt 8 times (total 80 rows). BO all sts.

Finishing

Place WS of both pieces tog and sew all around with a backstitch, leaving about 3" opening if stuffing pillow or 8" opening if using pillow form. Fold batting to size of pillow and insert into pillow, or insert pillow form. Sew opening closed.

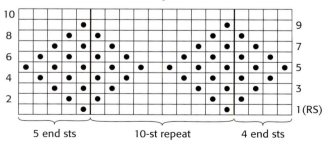

Baby Bunny Cuddle Toy

This bunny will be extra special when you knit it for your baby to love, cuddle, and drag around the house. It's washable and the eyes are stitched on—it'll last forever!

Skill Level
■■■□ Intermediate

Size
27" tall, with ears up

Materials
Yarn: 440 yards of worsted-weight superwash wool yarn (4)
Needles: Size 8 needles and size 8 double-pointed needles
Notions: Darning needle, small bits of yarn in contrasting color for face, stuffing

Gauge
18 sts and 24 rows = 4" in St st

Face
CO 49 sts. Work 12 rows in St st, ending with WS row.
Row 1 (RS): K5, K2tog; rep from * to end—42 sts.
Row 2 and all WS rows: Purl.
Row 3: *K4, K2tog; rep from * to end—35 sts.
Row 5: *K3, K2tog; rep from * to end—28 sts.
Row 7: *K2, K2tog; rep from * to end—21 sts.
Row 9: *K1, K2tog; rep from * to end—14 sts.
Row 11: K2tog to end—7 sts.
Row 12: Purl.
Cut a 12" tail and thread darning needle. Pull tail through rem 7 sts and pull tight. Bring sides tog to form cone shape and use thread tail to sew sides of cone tog, fasten off, and weave in ends.

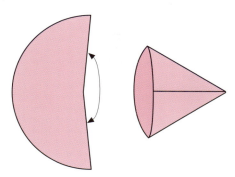

With darning needle and contrasting yarn, stitch eyes and nose in satin stitch. Stitch mouth as shown below.

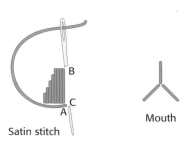

Satin stitch   Mouth

Back of Head
CO 16 sts (this is top of head). Working in St st, inc in middle of each knit row as follows:
Row 1: K8, K1f&b, K7—17 sts.
Row 2 and all WS rows: Purl.
Row 3: K8, K1f&b, K8—18 sts.
Row 5: K9, K1f&b, K8—19 sts.
Row 7: K9, K1f&b, K9—20 sts.
Row 9: K10, K1f&b, K9—21 sts.
Row 11: K10, K1f&b, K10—22 sts.
Row 13: K11, K1f&b, K10—23 sts.
Row 15: K11, K1f&b, K11—24sts.
Dec 1 st in middle of each knit row as follows:
Row 17: K11, K2tog, K11—23 sts.
Row 19: K10, K2tog, K11—22 sts.
Row 21: K10, K2tog, K10—21 sts.
Row 23: K9, K2tog, K10—20 sts.
BO 1 st at beg of every row until there are 9 sts.
BO all sts.

Ears (Make 4.)
CO 6 sts. Working in St st, inc 1 st in middle of each knit row until there are 18 sts.
Row 1 (RS): K3, K1f&b, K2—7 sts.
Row 2 and all WS rows: Purl.
Row 3: K3, K1f&b, K3—8 sts.
Row 5: K4, K1f&b, K3—9 sts.
Row 7: K4, K1f&b, K4—10 sts.

Row 9: K5, K1f&b, K4—11 sts.
Row 11: K5, K1f&b, K5—12 sts.
Row 13: K6, K1f&b, K5—13 sts.
Row 15: K6, K1f&b, K6—14 sts.
Row 17: K7, K1f&b, K6—15 sts.
Row 19: K7, K1f&b, K7—16 sts.
Row 21: K8, K1f&b, K7—17 sts.
Row 23: K8, K1f&b, K8—18 sts.
Dec 1 st in middle of each knit row until there are 8 sts.
Row 25: K8, K2tog, K8—17 sts.
Row 27: K8, K2tog, K7—16 sts.
Row 29: K7, K2tog, K7—15 sts.
Row 31: K7, K2tog, K6—14 sts.
Row 33: K6, K2tog, K6—13 sts.
Row 35: K6, K2tog, K5—12 sts.
Row 37: K5, K2tog, K5—11 sts.
Row 39: K5, K2tog, K4—10 sts.
Row 41: K4, K2tog, K4—9 sts.
Row 43: K4, K2tog, K3—8 sts.
*K2tog to end. Purl 1 row. Rep from * 2 more times. Pull yarn through and fasten off.

Chest
CO 20 sts. Working in St st, inc 1 st at each side of next 8 rows—36 sts.
Work in St st until chest meas 6¼".
Dec 1 st at each side every RS row 5 times—26 sts. Chest should meas approx 8".

Back
Work same as chest until back meas 6¼".
Work shaping as follows: K23, ssk, K1, turn. Sl 1, P11, P2tog, P1, turn.
Row 1: Sl 1 wyib, knit to gap, ssk (1 from each side of gap), K1.
Row 2: Sl 1 wyif, purl to gap, P2tog, P1.
Rep rows 1 and 2 until you have worked all sts. Work should meas approx 8". BO all sts.

Arms (Make 2.)
CO 20 sts. Work in St st for 8" and BO all sts.

Legs (Make 2.)
Using dpn, CO 24 sts and divide evenly over 3 needles (8 sts per needle). Join into rnd, pm, and work until leg meas 10".
Heel flap: K6, turn, and P12. (You'll now be working back and forth in rows.)

Row 1: Sl 1 pw wyib, knit to end.
Row 2: Sl 1 pw wyif, purl to end.
Rep rows 1 and 2 until 12 rows have been worked and there are 6 selvage sts on each side.
Turn heel: K7, ssk, K1, turn. Sl 1, P4, P2tog, P1, turn.
Row 1: Sl 1 wyib, knit to gap, ssk (one from each side of gap), K1, turn.
Row 2: Sl 1 wyif, purl to gap, P2tog, P1, turn.
Rep rows 1 and 2 until you have worked all sts.
Gusset: Knit across heel sts and PU 6 selvage sts. Knit across instep sts. With new needle PU 6 selvage sts.
Side to toe: *On needle 1, knit to last 3 sts, K2tog, K1. On needle 2, K1, ssk, knit to last 3 sts, K2tog, K1. On needle 3, K1, ssk, knit to end. Rep from * until there are 8 sts.
Graft toe with Kitchener stitch or cut yarn leaving long tail. Using darning needle, pull yarn tail through all stitches. Pull tight and fasten off.

Finishing
Weave in ends and sew pieces with RS tog as follows: Sew face to back of head, leaving small opening. Turn RS out.
Sew ears tog; then insert open end about 1" into inside of ear. Sew ears to top of head. Stuff head and sew up opening.
Stuff legs.
Sew up arms, leaving small opening. Stuff arms and sew up opening.

Position legs and arms against RS of back as shown and tack them down using basting stitch.

Place chest over top (legs will be sticking out of neck) and pin. Sew chest to back, making sure that legs and arms are firmly in place, and leave opening for turning. Turn RS out and stuff body. Position head on top of body and sew head to body.

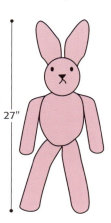

Knitting Abbreviations

[ ]	Work instructions within brackets as many times as directed.
( )	Work instructions within parentheses in the place directed.
*	Repeat instructions following the single asterisk as directed.
"	inch(es)
approx	approximately
beg	begin(ning)
BO	bind off
CC	contrasting color
CO	cast on
cont	continue
dec	decrease(ing)
dpn(s)	double-pointed needle(s)
EOR	every other row
est	established
foll	follow(ing)
inc(s)	increase(ing)(s)
K	knit
K1f&b	knit into front and back of same stitch—1 stitch increased
K2tog	knit 2 stitches together
K3tog	knit 3 stitches together
kw	knitwise
LH	left hand
M1	make 1 stitch
MB	make bobble
MC	main color
meas	measure(s)
mm	millimeter(s)
mo(s)	month(s)
P	purl

patt	pattern
P2tog	purl 2 stitches together
P3tog	purl 3 stitches together
pm	place marker
prev	previous
psso	pass slipped stitch over
p2sso	pass 2 slipped stitches over
PU	pick up and knit
pw	purlwise
rem	remaining
rep	repeat
RH	right hand
rnd(s)	round(s)
RS	right side(s)
sc	single crochet
SKP	slip 1, knit 1, pass stitch over the knit stitch—1 stitch decreased
S2KP	slip 2 stitches knitwise, knit 1, pass 2 slipped stitches over the knit stitch—2 stitches decreased
sl	slip
sl st	slip stitch
ssk	slip, slip, knit these 2 stitches together—a decrease
st(s)	stitch(es)
St st	stockinette stitch
tbl	through back loop
tog	together
WS	wrong side(s)
wyib	with yarn in back
wyif	with yarn in front
yd(s)	yard(s)
YO	yarn over

Helpful Information

Metric Conversion Chart

m	=	yds	x	0.9144
yds	=	m	x	1.0936
g	=	oz	x	28.35
oz	=	g	x	0.0352

Standard Yarn-Weight System

Yarn-Weight Symbol and Category Name	0 Lace	1 Super Fine	2 Fine	3 Light	4 Medium	5 Bulky	6 Super Bulky
Types of Yarn in Category	Fingering, 10-count crochet thread	Sock, Fingering, Baby	Sport, Baby	DK, Light Worsted	Worsted, Afghan, Aran	Chunky, Craft, Rug	Bulky, Roving
Knit Gauge Range* in Stockinette Stitch to 4"	33 to 40 sts	27 to 32 sts	23 to 26 sts	21 to 24 sts	16 to 20 sts	12 to 15 sts	6 to 11 sts
Recommended Needle in Metric Size Range	1.5 to 2.25 mm	2.25 to 3.25 mm	3.25 to 3.75 mm	3.75 to 4.5 mm	4.5 to 5.5 mm	5.5 to 8 mm	8 mm and larger
Recommended Needle in US Size Range	000 to 1	1 to 3	3 to 5	5 to 7	7 to 9	9 to 11	11 and larger

*These are guidelines only. The above reflect the most commonly used gauges and needle sizes for specific yarn categories.

What's your creative passion?

Find it at **ShopMartingale.com**

books • eBooks • ePatterns • daily blog • free projects
videos • tutorials • inspiration • giveaways